The Weight We Wear

AlexaBAD
Terri Boyd-Boone
Vita Gold
Rishawna L. Gould
Sophia Monet

Published By CC Miller, LLC
CCSaidThat.com

Copyright © 2025 by Terri Boyd-Boone, Rosalyn Chambers, Brittany Davis, JoVita Goldsby and Rishawna L. Gould.
Cover art Copyright © 2025 Terri Boyd-Boone.
All rights reserved. No part of this book may be reproduced or transmitted in any form or by any means, electronic or mechanical, including photocopying, recording, or by any information storage or retrieval system, without permission in writing from the copyright owners.

ISBN: 979-8-218-65627-0

Dedication

To our beloved friends and families who occupy the light and dark with us, this collection is for you. "The Weight We Wear" is the collective voice of five women, each navigating the mural of life through the lenses of love, loss, and resilience.

To those who have loved fiercely and lost profoundly, to those who forge their paths with strength, who balance dreams with duty, and redefine their narratives. Our stories are mirrored struggles and triumphs, a reminder that we are united in our experiences, and a celebration of the weight we carry together.

Table of Contents

Air	1
Ashes of the Unapologetic	2
Beneath the Hyde... Seek	5
Beware (Proverbs 7)	7
Freedom	9
Genius to Madness	11
gorda	14
Home Me	16
In Your Eye	17
Jesus Got Me Thinking	19
letting go	20
Listen to the Fire	22
PTSD	25
pushing past my crust	27
Sackcloth and Ashes	29
Say It Again, So I Believe You	32
Stripped	35
The Beast I Keep Locked In	36
The Echoes Before Hello	39
The Wait We Bear	43
The Weight Mistaken for Me	45
The Weight of Wings	48
Tulips	51
"You Still Sick?"	53
A Walk in the Rain	57
It Took Her. It Tried Me.	58
Gravity	62
Decisions	64

I'm Going to Paint Me A Picture	65
Force of Nature	67
Hands that Listen	68
Open Arms, Closed Doors	70
She	71
Watch Out for the Quiet Ones	73
Black-eyed Companion	76
For Bryan	78
Lukewarm	80
relief	82
Severed	84
She Let Him Hurt Me	85
For the One Who Stayed Up	89
missed	93
all weight ain't heavy	95
Daddy	97
big mama say	98
elephant's foot	100
Grits	101
Heirloom	103
if i should go	104
the weight we wear	107

Air

There's not enough air to relax these lungs
You knock the wind out of me
Far too young and too dumb to knock the fear out of me
So here we stand
About to fall
As I gasp for
air
I only ask that you care
Enough to let me go
Maybe then
I can capture the wind
I need to grow
Sophia Monet

Ashes of the Unapologetic

I am the cracks you see and the ones you don't.
Held together by duct tape and dreams,
Stitched with hopes too fragile to bear,
Glued together with words, unspoken but yearned for.

I give and I give, and I feel it all slip through my hands,
My time, my effort, my heart —
Yet the well runs dry, and I stand there,
Waiting for a reflection of my soul to return to me.

What if no one notices the weight I carry?
What if I disappear and the world continues on,
Unchanged, unbothered by my absence?
Who would miss the quiet hum of my spirit,
The echo of my sacrifices in the wind?

I need someone to say my name like it means something,
Like my existence matters,
Like my worth isn't measured by what I can give,
But by what I simply am.

I am tired.

Tired of being the giver, the fixer, the listener,
With no one to hold me when I fall,
No one to see the pieces scattered on the floor.

I need words—words that don't fall flat,
That wrap around me like a warm embrace.
I need to be seen, to be understood,
To be held in the way my heart has longed for.

But more than that,
I need to feel at home in this skin I wear,
To look in the mirror and see a woman,

Not a stranger who I'm trying to love,
But a woman who knows she's worthy
Of every ounce of affection,
Every tender touch she's been denied.

I need to stop doubting myself,
To find the strength I've buried deep inside.

Where is she?

That fierce, bold woman,
The one who doesn't apologize for existing,
The one who knows her worth without question.

She is buried beneath my fear,
Drowned by the noise of unmet needs,

But I will find her,
I will search every inch of myself
Until her voice rises from the ashes,
Until she speaks with a power I cannot deny.

I need affirmation.

Not as a plea, but as a birthright.
I need to believe I can stand tall in my truth,
Even when the world tries to shrink me down.
I need to stop fearing that I'll fail,

Stop fearing that my efforts will go unnoticed,
And instead, trust that my worth is not tied
To how much I give, but to how much I am,

Just as I am.
I am enough.

And I will learn to say it,
To feel it,
To believe it,
Until it flows from me like the breath of life.

Because in the end,
What I need most is not the validation of others,
But the courage to validate myself.
Rishawna L. Gould

Beneath the Hyde... Seek

(A Dialogue Poem - Excerpt)

How's your heart?

                                              How's your heart?

Is there wait on her?

                                             There's weight on her

She ticking? Or tricking
 you into believing she's still whole?

                                                 She trickster
                                      Want to know a secret?
                                    She was never really there

So there's a wait to be released
of every unfinished conversation
Every "I'm fine" lied through clenched teeth?

                             I am ellipsis... unfinished sentence
            Mannequin of memory draped in scraps of unspoken
                                    Patchworked shadows
                                          Survival couture

You call that living?

                                      Living Single-minded
                                  Living assistance by no one,
                                not even "sister," "sister"
                                      parody of presence

You didn't fit in?

                                           You didn't fit in
                                        Go big or go home
                    You built own House of Payne to live in

                                                   Hey you
                                              Yeah, you
                    What are you so afraid of anyway?

The truth?

                                                      The pain

Or is it me?
It's you.

Do I reflect what's real
Or project what you fear?

> I fear you reflect one you avoid like plague
> But feel more like prophecy
> Today and tomorrow's separation
> Anxiety

I'm not your enemy?

> You're not enemy
> I am evidence
> I am
> origin story
> Cloaked in shame
> barely breathing

Have I ever asked mind to swim deeper than heart
Instead of skimming shallow waters to avoid drowning in unrest?
Am I looking deep inside?

> What's inside of them

What's inside me?

> Beneath your Hyde...

Beneath my Hyde?
Am I using what He gave me as mirror, or only as sword
Reopening scars with words meant to set me free
Still blind to the light that could've healed me
Do I mask my mess as poetic or clothe synapsis in His depth?
No not death, no I'm not dead
Yet?

> Yet...

(Will I fight like Jacob limping with new name?)
> Want to know a█████? ... 🫢

AlexaBAD

Beware (Proverbs 7)

Time and time again she is warned of the wages of sin.
Guard her heart and let God's word be a chastity belt.
So onward she goes traveling on the road of life, able to resist temptations, but the Devil always has that one waiting up his sleeve.
You know that one who makes you catch your breath when he enters a room?
The one you can't believe has eyes for you, flashing his devilish smile
and wait a minute did he just shoot over a wink, too!
She tries to remember every scripture that forewarned of these desires as he saunters over, and within a few strides he's standing right in front of her.
Victim or prey in this moment, it's all the same as his viscous words of praise start to coat her inner strength.
He watches her fold little by little
countenance fading with each honey laced compliment.
Oh no! She's blushing
He's almost got her in his clutches.
The devil is in the background.
Hands clasped
Grinning
Thinking he's about to add another victim to his growing death toll.
He had a feeling this new dashing puppet would work this time;
he's saying all the right things and has this girl on the ropes.
Sweet words laced with poison spew from his lips, she's almost convinced
but before his words touch her heart
she remembers that the sweet waters he's offering lead to death.
He's starting to sound like the woman from Proverbs calling for stupid men to come into her awaiting den.
Promising unending pleasure without telling them the dire consequences once within.
She pauses his words to have a moment to shake her head free from his mental clutches
taking steps back giving them distance.
She opens her spiritual eyes to see what lies behind this man's disguise

just in the nick of time.
The Devil may have lost this round but as long as he has the time he will keep trying.
Beware and stay strong because they come in all shapes and sizes waiting for loneliness to shrink your resolve.

But she didn't listen

She now lies in a field of green clovers, her last breaths blending with the morning mist tears falling amongst the dew.
Her last thoughts wondering how she ended up here in this place?
Her lover's eyes will be the last things she sees.
In those eyes she once found peace
could drown in them forever.
They were warmer than a summer breeze.
In his eyes she saw life so clearly the world lay at their feet
her love blinded her true sight.
She wanted to only see the good so badly forgiving each time he blacked an eye or bruised a lip her forgiveness ran too deep.
In a field of clovers is where her luck will run and for the first time, she will notice the malice behind his eyes.
Knowing it was always there, turning a blind eye is now costing her life.
Last breath gone.
Last tear to be shed in a field of clovers being cleansed by the rain.
Vita Gold

Freedom

How can you tell someone they are a slave when they're not aware of the chains binding them to what's killing them?

How can you release someone who is aware but has become comfortable in the muck and mire that has plagued them either by choices or circumstances?

How can I tell someone to get free when my own burdens have shackled me in quicksand burying me alive gasping for air struggling for breath?

Inhale

How can I advise release when my own worries, guilt and struggles bind me to the cement on my feet, unable to move from this one spot ready to admit defeat?

When do I seek my own forgiveness and salvation to shed years of tears, regrets, sorrow and death?
How do I share freedoms when I'm not free myself?

Exhale

How do I reveal the secrets of hope when alone in the dark I feel hopeless and afraid of what the next day may bring continually in battle for my own salvation I beg for release from my own tragedy?

How do you forgive yourself when you have yet to forgive others for the damage they've caused, and the recklessness caused by oneself?

Inhale

The loneliest road is the one traveled to self-forgiveness.
Forgiving yourself for self-harm doing things the same knowing the results will be the same.

Forgiving oneself for doubting the strength you hold to finally break free from your own chains.

Exhale

Freedom is sometimes earned and not given once you realize you forgive yourself first then it will all start to make sense.
Vita Gold

Genius to Madness

Weight
lying in her every touch

She gets lost in the rhythmic beauty of melody with hopes that if she can't find herself,
maybe, neither can grief

Every ingenious note,
taking her an octave lower than
sanity

Harmony self-layered in dissonance
In a sense,
she beats self-up with own bars
off-key, adding insult to injury

Her cadence echoing progression to digression

Canon to her own crescendo
She plays sad song
that only her and the One who gifted her the power of song can hear

That's the CODA (of) honor
Written in Pure Treble
She plays at tempo too fast for self
Every notation adding sheets to her memoir
Every dynamic she had, the forte of learning to be lonely
The clef to low tone noting missed Chansons

Chances
To be
great

Guess that's just for tigers
Tony for wearing her stripes like red badge of honor

Honoring the scars of
Boxed memories
She never had a chance to unpack
Unpacking everything major
even when it seems minor

Takes courage.

Now, semitoned in
black excellence
till she gets it perfect
7th time's the charm,
No, the blessing
Triad of structures builds her foundation

Her worth never diminished
Even when internal conflict augmented

She sets her own scales

Written in His Staff,
her pitch has His signature
Her limits show no intervals

Weight lying in her every touch
She gets lost in the rhythmic beauty of melody, with hopes that if she can't find herself,
maybe, neither can grief

Every note,
taking her an octave lower than
sanity

He shifts the key
Modulation of mercy
Lifting her harmony from discord to grace

Rewriting her refrain of sorrow, composing crescendo of hope

Raising her higher than depths could pull her

She still has her moments, major and minor
He sustains the chord of her being

Till her song be
no longer of Dissonance but Redemption
AlexaBAD

gorda

i am hiding in plain sight
beneath fleshy burnt caramel skin
and lively smile you are accustomed to
coming around for a laugh or a hug
comfortable
warm
no risk
my fat is safe for you
and how with no worries i greet you
    in acquiescence actually but so turned down i don't
    even hear it anymore
my resistance more like a funny accent from my country that pops up
from time to time
but i am not from another place
like the place they called me gorda
another name for gorgeous
so i kept being told
but that's not here
but we can pretend
because another thing about my fat
it makes room for whatever
while i stay behind the curtain of my brown eyed windows
a safe nest high up inside my brain
like a Vouron Patra
well
until recently
when i looked into the mirror
i didn't recognize
myself
and wondered had i been fooling anyone else
or was the protection
i wore like a uniform
now stretched out like lycra that's seen the inside of the dryer too
many times
threadbare and cellulite bumpy

my fat that made it easy
now no longer easy
no distraction
only distortion
of how i see my own face
i feel myself sliding out of it's greasy hold
and you might think it's a good thing
to finally feel free
but it's terrifying really
what will hold people in place
near but at the isolating distance of this insulating fat
that the barrier between you and me
and me and me
is melting away
and i've never been so exposed
and raw
and scared
no coat cold
and nerve endings tingling
    and alive
        yes maybe alive
but
there is more to say
let's take this a day by day
one chubby poem at a time
Terri Boyd-Boone

Home Me

You home me
The grown me
I'm sick of the old me
The cold me
You unfold me
Try not to control me
Just be there to hold me
Home is where the start is
Home is where things get the darkest
Shades drawn, feet bare on the carpet
I lay across the bed
So much goes unsaid
So many books unread
Shelves covered in dust
Pictures covered in us
Trust be a little musty
Hint of rusty
But we don't cave
Is this the way love behaves
Sophia Monet

In Your Eye

See me, Jehovah, the way I want to see myself so I can become the person you need me to be.
Show me the reason you chose me to remind me of the goodness in my heart I feel may be
lacking.
Show me, oh Jehovah, the way I should walk because my steps have led me from
one tragic ending to another and the light at the end of the tunnel I've created for myself has
gone black as a starless night.
Lead me from my heart and the demands it brings for her treachery knows no bounds and only you can save me from...me.
My own devices lead to heavy prices so please save me from death's grip.
Loosen the noose this world has tied twice
around my neck
playing hangman day to day and there are not enough letters in any language's alphabet to save me from the impending shipwreck.
Only you, oh Jehovah, can save me from
certain calamity.
This is my psalm that I pray into heavy palms soaked with tears and fears
My only rescue is to hear my prayers.
Look at me as the pupil of your eye battling life's crimes until
the day I can leave it all behind.
Keep my feet firm and my faith steady
getting out of my own way to make your heart glad rejoicing saying see this one finally made it.
I am here, oh Jehovah,
see me.
Clear my path from past debris so I can experience your love whole-souled completely
free.
I am here and yours, oh Jehovah, please send me yes, send me so I can be the woman you

need me to be.
In your eyes, Jehovah, is the only place I want to be.
Forgive me.
Vita Gold

Jesus Got Me Thinking

Jesus has me thinking, am I worthy of his sacrifice?
Will I ever live up to anything close to the
perfect example he's laid out and died to give?
Will I get to be one percent as compassionate
with myself as I'm to be with those I preach to?
Will I ever give myself the grace that he was
willing to give so many?
Will I be patient with me as he was with the apostles when they faltered even in his most desperate time of need?
I pray to not make his death in vain and to conquer these inner demons of doubt.
To push forward because his life matters to me.
Yeah, Jesus got me thinking to
be a better version of me.
Vita Gold

letting go

back in the day
my Momma and her friends
celebrated forty like new years
saying it was their best year
a new life
no more fear

me being in the throes of the 1st life crisis
not yet knowing this current self and its faces
of self esteem
  self respect
    self care
instead it was self sabotage
self doubt
  self neglect
    myself awkward and insecure
      i knew those faces
the bookshelves of great selves of 14 or 15
full of sad songs and poetry
how they ride your back as you leave your tweens
stuffed down like delinquent homework
in a pink backpack
a journal full of secret wishes
showing up like a scrunchie after a short haircut
making you regret changes in favor of old familiar ways

so i waited for forty
weighted with these former versions of me
because i was a sucker for a good abandonment story
and forty must have passed by like an express bus/ out of service/
heading for the station
myselves distracted me like
children crying because they were hungry
and they were famished
for attention

   for approval
     for acceptance
so i sat like a single mother
waiting for my good year man

and off in the distance of fifty
i realized these kids weren't even mine
like an adopted thinking
fostering in my head

and they had a daddy

he could have them
he was the father of the lies
i had told myself

letting go came with tears
I try not to get sentimental when i stumble over a discarded teddy bear

i am finally living in my best year
Terri Boyd-Boone

Listen to the Fire

I wrote it rough, drafted
in a pear of ideals
Meant for their eyes
When,
it wasn't even meant for mine.

I...chipped...away
at its core
till words began to take shape
Freshly from earth
Dug from resistance - past decorum
Every jagged edge
Heavy with meaning

Hiding
its fire
 Its brilliance,
Unrealized, but
weighty.

Listen to the Fire

Waiting
for clarity
Each facet
telling the story of
every blemish for which I sought atonement
Characterizing my identity

 Listen to the Fire
I
cannot grade a head I
never took the time to crown.

Listen to the Fire

Mining for depth leads to
Raw
Beginnings,
Unearthing pieces of **me, I...forgot...I...buried**

Suddenly I wasn't trying to polish the pain, but
hold it to the light
Ready to listen,
to the colors dancing off the melody
of the luminescence that
Hits
It
Just
Right

Listen to the Fire

I hold my poem to the sun, turn It slowly
as sorrow refracted
Staring through this prism of understanding,

                      Truth
              lit up like sparks
        on glass, igniting the **Sun's**
      beauty—reflecting **Son's beauty**,
that set to raise me above simulant standards.
I saw where **Pain** glimmered, clutching onto right hand of **Hope**,
where **Love** burned while nestled quietly in a corner —**Purpose**,
        searching for **Desire**—
    Fire, breathing life into **Essence, Essence,**
            restless,
      reaching for **Self**-expression—
         Self-expression
           expressing

Now,
If only I would stop trying to force you into a shape
you were never meant to be
Listening to the fire consuming someone else's reality...

Listen to the Fire

I cannot control my environment, but I can control my shine so,
I chiseled, not to tame
but to set it free
An emerald cut for clarity
A cushion for the tender parts, enhanced by heart
Radiant in grown qualities from the image I was naturally created to reflect
Colored in strength
A princess cut to crown the ache of the unspoken
Treating natural instincts
with dignity
Gleaming
Not perfect
But honest
Not polished into silence
Carved to catch fire
When they read it, they see the shine
Not the dust
of what used to be treasure

Where is your fire?
AlexaBAD

PTSD

I was bound to you as soon as I was found by you just to turn around and be drowned by you
Realizing I'm traumatizing myself
My biggest trauma bond is the one that began when I was too young to ask for help
Attention seeking
People pleasing
Because you made me uncomfortable with myself

Must have been something in the water that day
Because you couldn't simply walk away
We will be connected until we are perfected
I will be affected as long as I'm not protected
Even as the physical fades, the mental it plays, in ways I can't explain

I flashed back
Lost track of time
I'm not 4
I'm not 9
But I find myself right back there in that chair with that stare
Life can be so unfair

Eyes still glazed over
When will this all be over
When will I be free from your grips
Whiplash
No take backs

I accept your apology
But it doesn't mean it hasn't got to me
Two steps forward
Another set back
The clocks sets back

1990

No need to remind me
You always manage to find me
You have the worst timing

Ball and chain
This vision imprisoned in my brain
Why do you confine me?

Restricted
To one visit
To one instance
How
Can one instance
Define me
Define us
Define trust

This is
To pay homage
To those still in bondage
To the abused
Left confused
There is light at the end of the tunnel
Sophia Monet

pushing past my crust

my Daddy used to say
TMac you always get clumsy
before you grow

this morning
as i drop the breakfast ingredients
one by one on the floor
i epiphanied
these are the days for growing
pushing past my crust
exposing what's been seeding
in the soil
in the dark

in my consternation i demand
where is it happening
these spurts of mine
mind you
i've been the same height since 4th grade
and i am still banging into table edges
and dropping things on my feet

it must be in my spirit
how my heart and mind keep
blooming taller
expanding beyond current foliage
and sprouting higher in the philosophy of me
from photosynthesis of Scripture and meditation
my Jehovah gives advice with his eye on me
It comes through conversations with those who care deeply
for the whole of all my parts
in a talk before the end of an Assembly
a fertilization a pruning
a transplanting so the sunlight can bathe my branches
and water will find my roots

i am about to flower

so when Clumsy comes with it's familiar song
i prepare myself for wider girthing
this call and response of growing
it's coming
in a low tone voice
above field hollers and hymns for my harvest

it's coming

a voice
usually my own
a truth voice
simple and clear
that gives new answers to old questions

it's coming
and i wait for it
sometimes bruised
often exhausted
always excited

for the next understanding of me
  Terri Boyd-Boone

Sackcloth and Ashes

I vomited
I couldn't stomach it
My God's face turned away
As I closed my eyes to pray

I felt nothing

Nothing but the contents of my bowels echoing through the silence

Nauseous

Spiritual sickness at its thickest
Stiff neck
Quick to reject counsel

"Turn around
Please
Repent in sackcloth and ashes"

I walk right past it
In complete opposition
Stood in the position of disobedience
I couldn't see that it
Was me
Who had become so distant, cold, and hardhearted
Disregarded my inheritance
In the mirror, I would stare at it
My face
Replaced
By a heathen
Believing I could keep breathing poisonous air while occupying a chair at his table

Disrespectful

He told me He would hold me accountable
For my sins He would extend mercy
But the punishment would hurt me
My bones would quake
My heart would shake
My core couldn't ignore disciplinary action

To feel just a fraction of His dissatisfaction took my breath away
In lamentation I had a revelation

A vision of humility

See, He had humbled me to the fullest degree
To be scolded by the oldest living being in the universe
Let me tell you, it hurts
It burns
It turns your insides out
From my intestines, I'd shout

"Father, please!"

On my knees I'd plead for restoration through supplication and thanksgiving

"Life ain't worth living without you
Take my hand once again and let my feet land on solid ground

Father, please!

Catch sight of me as I extend all energy
As I run to get to you
I pray you meet me halfway"

That very day He reached out His hand and my heart began to breathe again
Undeserved kindness from spiritual blindness to sheer delight

At the sight of His gifts in men
Greased with the finest of oils
The scent sent to the heavens a triumphant noise
The earth below rejoiced

"Here I stand before you
Never again will I ignore you
And your righteous decrees
May every knee on earth and heaven bend

Thank you, Father!
Thank you, Father, for bringing me home again"
Sophia Monet

Say It Again, So I Believe You

I don't love myself—
not yet.
But don't confuse that with weakness.
Don't mistake my silence
for surrender.

Pause.

I was raised on humility,
fed scraps of praise
like I had to earn oxygen.
Dad, the first man in my life, kept his compliments
like they were gold coins—
and I was never rich enough
to deserve one.

So yeah—
I flinch when someone calls me beautiful.
Look away, laugh it off,
like maybe if I reject it first,
it won't hurt so bad
when it's taken back.

I am fat.
Big bellied Bertha.
Bat wings.
Thunder thighs.
A walking punchline
in someone else's joke.
But this body?

This body *stayed*.
When people didn't.
When my hair didn't.
When my health didn't.

This body carried pain
and still got up.
Still walked through fire
with no applause,
no camera flashes—
just grit
and a tired kind of grace.

And I may not be J-Lo,
Beyoncé,
or whatever the world calls "worthy"—
but I'm still here.
Still aching to believe
that heads can turn for me, too.
That maybe one day
I'll see myself
and not want to hide.

I want to strut,
to swing these hips
like they were made
to

I want to laugh so loud
my insecurities crawl back
into the holes
they came from.

I want to stare at my reflection
and not just tolerate her—
but **honor** her.
Fall for her.
Hold her like a lover
who never walks away.
(beat – then strong, grounded)

Because she?
She's been through **hell**.
She's carried silence,
shame,
sickness—

and still dares
to dream
of beauty.

Tell me that's not fierce.
Tell me that's not art.
Tell me that's not
already
enough.
Rishawna L. Gould

Stripped

Standing before this mirror naked
I no longer like what I see.
Seeing the truth has set me free and now I have to strip off this old personality.
Decades and decades of debauchery and sin, things I never realized were slowly killing me.
I begin to rip and pull.
Stretching and tearing into rotten flesh discarding old sins along with old whims.
Desperately clawing to get to the new me these old flesh wounds try just as hard to cling to me.
Struggling literally fighting for my life.
Pounds of flesh hit the floor thudding like bricks.
I never knew I was carrying so much spiritual dead weight.
With each layer I feel new life breathing through.
A moth emerging from her cocoon spiritual freedom is right at the dawn.
With each pound cast off I pray to get the same in spiritual redemption.
Jah, give me your spirit to put on your spiritual armor to protect me from me.
Stepping away from the old me feeling brand new I look back into the mirror, my new armor glistening brighter than every morning sun.
I raise my hands in thanks, grateful to be stripped free of the old personality.
Vita Gold

The Beast I Keep Locked In

I'm quiet.
Soft-spoken.
Bruce Banner in the daylight,
just trying to walk humbly,
keep my peace,
and stay out of the storm.

But inside me,
there's a storm brewing.
A woman—
a she-Hulk—
locked in chains,
waiting.
Watching.
Quiet,
dormant,
but never gone.

It takes a lot to wake her.
A lot.
But you don't know that.
You don't know the fire inside me
that builds,
slowly,
until it's ready to break free.
And when she is unleashed,
there's no turning back.
She doesn't ask for permission.
She doesn't care for your reasons.
She will burn the world down,
and I'll watch,
helpless,
hoping she'll stop.

But I don't want her to come out.

I don't want the rage
to flood my veins,
to turn me into someone I can't recognize.

I don't want to be that woman—
the one who breaks things,
hurts things,
becomes the destruction she's been avoiding.

And so I pray.

Jehovah,
help me hold her in.
Help me breathe through the fire
before it consumes me.

Give me strength
to keep the Hulk at bay,
to keep my peace,
to keep my calm.
For I know,
when she's released,
I will lose more than control—
I'll lose myself.

But every day,
people test my Hulk.
Every day,
they push.
They prod.
They push me closer to the edge
until I'm standing on the line
between peace and chaos.

Jehovah,

I need You now.
I need Your patience,
Your grace,
Your mercy,
to keep this Hulk inside.

Don't let me break.
Don't let me snap.
Guide my steps when the world
wants me to fall apart.

Hold me,
Jehovah,
hold me tight
so that I don't become the monster
I'm so afraid of.

Please,
just today—
let me stay Bruce.
Just today—
let me walk in peace.
And tomorrow…
I'll pray again.

Rishawna L. Gould

The Echoes Before Hello

Hi there!
...Nah.
That's not what I wanna say.
Might scare him away
before I even get the chance to say...

Hey.

Or better yet—
like Lionel once said,
"Hello? Is it me you're looking for?"

God, I *wish*.

Then I wouldn't have to sit in this abyss,
this echoing silence
that strips the bliss from me
when all I want—
all I've *ever* wanted—
is to be seen.

For so long,
I've lived invisible.
Camouflaged in the shadows of louder women,
bolder women,
"look-at-me" women.

And me?
I miss my moment.
I miss my chance.
I miss my shot.
Because shyness?
Shyness is a full-body paralysis
disguised as humility.
But I just wish—

God, I wish—
that he could see me.

See me
through the ocean of sisters
that stretch the whole earth wide—
and still reach for *me*.

That he might glance across the room,
just once,
with that kind of look—
that "I see you in a crowd of everyone" look—
and say,
"There she is."
My future.
Written in the stars
before either of us even knew how to read the signs.
But time keeps ticking.
And my mind?
Sometimes it spirals.
Overthinking into oblivion.
Going insane in the membrane,
worrying about things
that haven't even become reality yet.
Still, I wish he could see me.
See me
not for what I possess,
but for *who* I am.
See my heart,
stimulate my mind,
stir my thoughts
like sugar in morning coffee.
Seduce my intellect
with words that whisper,
"You are worth knowing."

Give me reason to believe
that being soft
isn't a weakness—
but a doorway
into something sacred.
But days pass.
Weeks.
Years.

Hellos come and go.

And these bandages?
They hold my heart together like worn thread.
But I'm okay.
I'm okay
because I pray.
I say,
**"Lord, here I am.
Send him."**
Airmail.
Snail mail.
Message in a bottle.
I don't know.
But You do.
You know the road
that leads to me.

So I stay.
Still.
Soft.
Hopeful.

I wait for the one who'll stay—
not just show up,
but *build*.

Build something that doesn't crack when tested.
Something rooted,
grounded,
whole.

And if he never comes?
If he loves me not?
I still wait.
Patiently.

Because I know—
my heart is worth the seeing.
And one day,
someone will look my way
and finally say:
**"There you are.
I see you."**
Rishawna L. Gould

The Wait We Bear

I often stare into the distance
By that, I mean the future
A world complete
Grass beneath my feet

See, my current residence isn't pleasant
It's more disengaging
A world that's raging war within itself
So, I carry my shield and wait for help

Wait for peace

See, underneath my belief is sheer fear that I won't survive
Despite my fright, I stay along for the ride
Try to keep pace in the race
Yet, I fear I'm falling behind

This shield feels like steel

Still, I stand erect waiting for Him to interject
I reflect on His promises made
I watch the way He behaves
The way that He moves
His chariot, he carries it along

I follow along while praising through song
Glory be to God

Glory weighs a lot
He wears it well

As he carries his wait
For vindication and salvation of a nation of righteous ones

His eyes in the direction of a resurrection of those he loves

Our desires intertwined as my brother comes to mind
Waiting in anticipation for the moment he will awaken
The ground will be moved
The earth will be shaken
On the day of realization

As I ponder on wonders yet beheld
I stare into the distance

Awaiting a new existence
One free from sickness
From a mind tormented
Fragments of shame, guilt, and repentance

Soon this wait will be lifted
Gifted with the richest sacrifice
Freed for everlasting life
In exquisite delight
I put down the darkness and pick up the light
Sophia Monet

The Weight Mistaken for Me

The doormat scowls as
my heart knocks at ribs
like unwelcomed guest in own home
Throbbing loud enough for the silence to side-eye me

It creaks open from inside handle
Wanting to swing wide to something
Familiar
Afraid the floor is lava

I step in with hands unclenched
Hoping that you see me not as foe, but friend
Your quiet rises like smoke from
fire I didn't set

Stare
Sharp as history lessons I always avoided
Cuts me to core to wear shadow of those that wanted to dim your light
My supplication to He
pleading that they never succeed rises like sweet incense, with incentive to not lose your sweet incense

I proceed with caution
Reminding myself: you were dropped by hands that taught you caution
Not mine

Your eyes half-closed shutters
I shudder
As you peer through me
You see me,
But do you see my fear? Of losing you?

Though I wear no scent of danger,
you inhale me like warning

I choke
Missing those breaths you hold hostage every time I speak

Your fear tugging at my name,
misspelling my presence,
calls me stranger when I came in peace

I know it's not you,
so I
Stay

Even though my trauma whispers:
"Maybe it is me"

How heavy it is
to be a canvas for your pain,
I try so hard not to cause

To be green with envy for those that receive your friendship gift-
wrapped, not in doubt
Blue from circumstance
Red from the crimes a scene
Post memories unjust
From a system too broken to hold truth

Guilty of association? Or existence?

I smile like I don't feel every flinch you never meant to show,
and breathe relief each time your shell softens,
revealing the glisten of the real you

I remain
unfolding quietly,
a softness unburned,
hoping one day you'll see
this heart,

this pulse,
this me
This love
As one that doesn't fail
not the echo of harm,
but the one trying to be an answer to it

Why? Because your friendship is worth it
AlexaBAD

The Weight of Wings

Life of an Empath
I was born with open hands
and a heart that heard whispers
most never noticed.
They called me *"too much"*—
"too soft", "too sensitive", "too kind",
as if feeling deeply were a flaw
I hadn't yet grown out of.

"Be tougher," they'd say.
"Be louder. Fight back."
But I wasn't made for armor.
I was made for sensing storms
in other people's skies
and offering shelter
even when mine was crumbling.

I didn't know what I was
until the word *empath*
wrapped itself around my truth—
a soul tuned to frequencies
that others ignore,
a vessel that absorbs
the pain and the joy
of those who never asked me to carry them.

Yes, it's heavy.
Yes, some days I'd give anything
to just *not* feel—
to turn the volume down
on everyone else's hurt
and rest inside my own.
But the gift is not in escape—
it's in endurance.

It's in the soft resilience
of loving anyway.

We are the healers,
the encouragers,
the ones who see
past the masks.
And sometimes that sight
draws wolves in disguise—
the takers, the users,
the charmers who twist
our compassion into currency.

But I've learned.
I'm learning.
Boundaries are not walls—
they are bridges to peace.
And loving myself
is not selfish—
it's sacred.

This gift is a fire
and I've burned,
but I've also lit the way
for others lost in dark places.
What a miracle it is—
to feel so much
and still choose to give.

So call me too much.
Call me tender.
I'll wear those words like armor now.
Because I've got wings made of empathy
and a spine made of grace.
I may carry the world some days—
but I'm learning to carry myself too.

And oh, how brightly
I was meant to shine.
Rishawna L. Gould

Tulips

Tulips—such a beautiful creation of burden.
You burden me with your ability
to welcome the light,
to beautify a room even in the presence of shade

I had just begun to embrace my fate, with these four white walls as my confidants—
but now you confidently
consume my oxygen,
as if this room were big enough for both of us

You steal my attention
when my attention was meant for me

Now my self-care is caring that while you sit well-watered,
my mind is parched with memories
of all the times I lacked refreshment

How is it that when you close
to protect yourself from the cold,
you are not judged as cold?

Why do they accept your isolation
but not mine?

Your bloom has me growing in jealousy
Your bulb lights my remorse,
cornering me in regret
And now, in the present,
I lie cornered still,
because your brightly colored accents
refuse to let me ignore your presence—
springing me into Great Depression

Tulips—such a beautiful creation of burden

Why do you insist on unemploying my peace?
AlexaBAD

"You Still Sick?"
(A Spoken Word Roundhouse Kick to the Clueless)

They say:
"When will you get better?"
Like healing comes with a receipt.
Like I picked out a two-week cold,
But they accidentally gave me the deluxe mystery illness package.

"You're sick again?"
Yep—my body's got commitment issues.
Keeps breaking down without warning.
No loyalty. No warning lights. Just chaos.

"Still not better?"
Still.
As if recovery works like microwave popcorn—3 minutes, done.

"You don't look sick."
And you don't look like an expert in anything,
But here we are.

"Did you go to the doctor?"
No, I just consulted the neighborhood squirrel.
Of course I went to the doctor.

"What did the doctor say?"
Oh, the usual—
"Hmm."
"Interesting."
"Let's run more tests."
"Could be stress."
Translation: We don't know squat.
But hey, it's in a white coat, so it must be divine wisdom, right?

"Well, the doctor should know."
Oh right! I forgot doctors are omniscient now.
Built my body, named my organs,
Attended the board meeting when my DNA was assigned.
Silly me—for thinking I might understand my own pain better than a clipboard.

"Just drink water."
Because clearly, I've been surviving on sand.

"Maybe just walk around the block."
Right.
With these joints? These lungs? This soul made of wet concrete?
I'll crawl the block—how's that?

"It's probably stress."
Everything is stress when you're not listening.

"Push through it."
If I push any harder, I'll collapse.
I'm not lazy—I'm carrying invisible weight
While y'all throw bricks of advice like it's helpful.

"It's all in your head."
And you are all up in my business.
Neither of y'all are invited.

"You were fine yesterday."
And guess what?
The weather was sunny yesterday, too.
Now it's storming. **That's life.**

Then they pivot.
New topic. Same clueless energy.

"Are you still single?"
Yeah—because I don't hand out front-row seats
To people who can't handle the show.

"You'll find someone."
Maybe.
But until then, I'm not lowering the volume
To make anyone comfortable in my presence.

"It's easy to lose weight. Just do it."
Oh?
Did you skip the part where I'm battling exhaustion, pain, and hormones in protest?
I must've missed the episode where discipline overruled biology.

"All you need is consistency."
All you need is to sit this one out.

"Your grief will pass."
Will it?
Because mine pulled up with a suitcase
And redecorated my life in shades of gone.

Here's the truth:
Your words don't comfort.
They don't fix.
They don't see me.

They decorate your discomfort
With fake empathy and recycled advice
And call it kindness.

If you don't know what to say—**don't**.

Bring snacks.
Bring silence.

Bring presence.
But don't bring your ego wrapped in concern.

Because I'm not your teachable moment.
I'm not your *"feel better soon"* experiment.
I am surviving—in real time.
And your questions?
They're a pop quiz I never asked for.

So next time your mouth opens,

Ask yourself:
Is it compassion...
or just noise?

Because I've got enough of that
Already
Screaming
Inside me.
Rishawna L. Gould

A Walk in the Rain

Today, I walked outside with no umbrella because the rain hasn't fallen in a while and my tears
have been locked up so I took this moment to shed a few.
I let the showers cleanse my soul it was as if in this moment Jehovah was washing away all the
stress and anxiety of this world.
Yes, it rains upon sinner and saint alike
but today, this sinner needed a deep clean.
With each step and tear I released every burden.
I went by each sin one-by-one
this was going
to turn into more than a stroll but a journey.
What started as a light rain turned into a tempest reflecting my inner pain my emotions and
weather in sync *sorry to anyone else who stepped outside today.*
The tears fall,
my heartbeat thundered,
my crying out strikes like lightning begging to be saved.
I think I picked the wrong day to come outside.
I think The Almighty could hear his child reaching out because through the storm clouds the sun
began trying to make its way through
fighting all the hurt and pain of this weary soul.
Its rays reach for me like a father trying to hug a child.
I reach back to accept the warmth.
As soon as we touch, peace takes over the rain and my tears begin to subside.
I turn my face to His glory letting Him heal my broken spirit and renew my fractured faith.
Today, I walked outside with no umbrella to let the rain blend with my tears only to find my biggest fear
was if Jehovah left me.
He showed me that He will always be there to carry me through.
Vita Gold

It Took Her. It Tried Me.

It came like a thief.
Unseen.
Uninvited.
It tore through everything—
my sense of safety,
my body,
my history.

But before it ever reached me,
it came for her.

My mother.

The strongest person I've ever known.
One stroke.
Then another.
Then more.

Until she was no longer the woman who raised me,
but the shell of someone fighting to stay here.

The stroke robbed her.
Robbed me.
Robbed us.

It didn't just take her movement.
It took her light.
Her laughter.
The sound of her voice saying my name.
The safety I only ever found in her presence.

Gone.

It stripped her piece by piece—
like some wicked hand peeling back the layers

of a life she built with strength and grace.
And I could only watch.

Helpless.
Angry.
Raging inside at the injustice of it all.

She didn't pass gently.
She was taken.
Plundered.

And before the grief could even settle,
the same thief came for me.

I knew it the moment it hit—
the confusion,
the spinning,
the numbness,
the sense that my own body
was betraying me in real time.

I had seen this horror show before.
I knew how it ended.
But I refused.
I raged.
Not in fear—
but in defiance.

I raged like a wild animal backed into a corner—
howling in silence,
trapped in a body that wouldn't obey.
I screamed without sound,
beat the walls inside my own mind,
clawed at the pieces of myself slipping away.

I cursed the stroke.

Cursed the thief.
Cursed the timeline of pain I never asked for.

I raged because I knew exactly what was happening.
I'd seen it eat her alive.
And now it wanted me.

I punched the air.
I wept into pillows until they were soaked and raw with grief.
I shook with fury in hospital beds,
in hallways,
in the quiet moments between tests,
when no one could see the fire burning through my chest.
I raged because I was still here—
but everything felt stolen.
And I was not going to let it happen again.

Even when my body collapsed,
even when my speech broke,
when my thoughts betrayed me,
I held on.

By a thread.
By a breath.
By the memory of the woman it had already stolen.

And even as my fists clenched in fury,
God never let go.
He was there in the silence.
In the rehab.
In the doubt.
In the tiny victories that felt like miracles—
standing, speaking, living.

He held me when I couldn't hold myself.
When I wanted to quit.

When the weight of grief and recovery crushed me to the floor.

But I didn't quit.

I survived the storm that took her.
I rose from the same wreckage that buried her.
I still miss her with a pain that burns.
I still cry for what was stolen.
But I stand.
Not untouched.
Not unscarred.
But undefeated.
The thief came.
It tried to finish what it started.

But I am still here.

Not because I won easily.
But because I fought with everything in my soul.
When I thought I had nothing else, I relied on faith.
Because grace carried me through the fire.

She lost the battle.
I carry the war.

And this—
this life,
this healing,
this breath—
is mine.
Rishawna L. Gould

Gravity

Sunrise over majestic skies
Under
Heavenly bodies
The gravity of reality
Pulling me to humility
And patience

Just when I thought I couldn't take it
My senses were awakened
There are only two options
Life or death

To live is to give
Praise
In ways made from sacrifices
Until there is nothing left
But the purest of worship

We are sparrows
With marrow
Composed of imperfection
Yet set free from the molecular matter which we refer to as sin
Renewing the person within

New beginnings
Start with
Sunset
Endings
Bread
Wine
And divine direction

As I stare into my reflection
Witnessing my faith's resurrection

He bought me back to life
Sophia Monet

Decisions

Decisions come with precision, but distractions come with infractions that cause the brain to have contractions worse than labor pains.

A strain that stops all plans in its tracks.
Those distractions can be doubt, anguish, and frustration.
The mental capacity to deal with it all is crippling.
Plans unfulfilled are a curse to a free spirit.

Nothing worse than to be trapped by one's own mind.
Vita Gold

I'm Going to Paint Me A Picture

I'm gonna paint me a picture of my ideal man
A one-of-a-kind original that no one else can

Something Rembrandt, Picasso or Van Gogh couldn't master
I know what I want, and I can paint faster

First, I'll start with a large canvas so grand—
Mmm, I've got goosebumps as I picture this man.

Got my palette ready and my brushes laid out,
Acrylic, watercolor? Hmmm... Oil no doubt.

He'll be the talk of the town, the envy of all,
A creation of love, my heart's final call.

I'll use vanilla cream or Hershey brown for the base,
And mix hues of caramel to contour his face

As I add strokes of sepia to outline his form,
I picture this man, a vision reborn;

With features divine, a silhouette bold,
A timeless creation, both gentle and gold.

Adorned with humility, kindness, and grace,
A reflection of virtues no paint can replace.

A man whose love is untainted and pure,
A partner in life, who is steadfast and sure.

I'll paint him a heart that knows no deceit,
A love that begins the moment we meet.

Next, I'll add clothes - a tough decision to make
Formal? Casual? Can't make a mistake.

A crisp white tee and some blue jeans will do,
Timbs on his feet, my select choice of shoe.

One last stroke and my man is complete –
Beautifully made, yet he lacks a heartbeat

The one beat that I long to feel;
A beat that only God could make real.

A mouth he has, but no words to say,
Eyes that gleam, but can't look my way.

Here he stands, perfection in art,
But a 2D man can't capture my heart.

I admire from afar, though he's so close to see,
For touching the paint would ruin him for me.

Oh, if he were flesh, with warmth and might,
To hold me close through the coldest of nights.

But until that time, I sit patiently and wait
For the real-life version of my painted soul mate.
Rishawna L. Gould

Force of Nature

Of course, they're going to be offended while they are still lying to themselves
and you're living His truth

Truthfully, they stifle their own growth
trying to round up your flowers as if weeds to their existence
You don't exist to fit their garden
Don't let them bury you in doubt and call it landscaping
They'd rather rip out your fine-soiled roots than repent from their rot
hardened by rocky ground and system-fed drought

What they sow
they shall reap
As will you

Real Efforts Aids Progress

So let them frown at your bloom
Let your roots run wild from their concrete expectations
Break the mold of the pot they tried to keep you in

You are not ornamental, you are original
Origin in the Father that cannot lie
A force of nature,
to be reckoned with
Not a fixture of their design, dependent on their time and attention
to water your ego
so you don't wilt beneath their condemned hopes

When they call your growth rebellion
Tell them survival always looks like resistance

And beauty rarely asks for permission
AlexaBAD

Hands that Listen

You arrived knotted
Nodes of stress
Dense
Woven into muscle mass massing pent-up emotion
Emoting the things you don't confess, express

Perplexed

Tension hidden beneath practiced smile
I greet you
First-name basis

You hesitate
Then hand overweight you didn't realize you had been carrying for too long

The room quiet

Your body speaks loudly

Telling story of sleepless nights in bed, waking up on wrong side of it
Unspoken arguments
Losses
Lack of hydration from the days your self wasn't caring enough to nourish a beautifully molded vessel

Listening with my palms
I release pieces you buried

Till your shoulders sink a little deeper
Tissue for the untreated memories
Tracing scars with respectful fingers
Till Baring more than surface value

Ambience serenades you

The world still in turmoil
 Yet the heart, open-armed, welcomes peace
The mind, wary of strangers, peeks from the corner
longing to trust
Peace slips in through the backdoor,
until the heart beats in arrhythmic tones,
trying to match calm's steady stride
Slowly, you separate from the system's demands

Stress whispers lies
I pass superficial
Massage pain
Soothe friction
Knead regret, till I trigger points of view that ring true

Grief grips spine, but
Tension reveals truth

You flinch when I find it
I breathe deeper until your essence follows
A conversation without questions
A trust earned in silence
I feel that exact moment you stop masking suppression as strength

Softness,
new and real,
reveals transparency
And you, finally,
embody
the nerve to heal
AlexaBAD

Open Arms, Closed Doors

It was a relief to let go of
ones that never deserved free access,
who mistook open arms for open season
Armed with malice
Opened fire on my confidence till I bled distrust
Used my own internal conflict to disarm my safety

Rusty but still forged from tough metal
I reclaimed the keys to my peace,
changed the locks on borrowed time,
and watched silence do the work
my words could never finish
AlexaBAD

She

She is not one of many but one of one.
The sun rises when she smiles.

In her eyes lies the truest of her being.
Her shoulders are heavy with the weight of the world on her cape.
She walks as if on clouds, her toes feathers but, if you could see the bottoms of her feet, you would see the scrapes and tears from the cape she wears
and the sun still rises when she smiles.

Look how straight her back may seem.
How strong like a red oak tree but, what you don't see is the cracking of her knees bearing the load of so many

and the sun still rises when she smiles.

Her arms are strong, each one holding a metric ton. One for her worries the other for her triumphs but, look at her elbows growing weary by the day her fight goes on

and still the sun rises when she smiles.

Her legs are like steel standing tall and proud.
She's made it this far by the sweat of her brow but, look at her knees ready to buckle and scream from carrying all of this weight with one strong wind she just might break

and still the sun rises when she smiles.

One may ask how does she do it?
How come she hasn't folded from the pressure?
The answer would be it's her heart that keeps it all going on.
It's the power source that keeps her engine running steadfast and sure.
It keeps her vision straight to stay on her course.
It oils any and all of her rusty parts.

Yes, it's her heart that keeps her from falling apart

and the sun still rises when she smiles.
Vita Gold

Watch Out for the Quiet Ones

They say,
watch out for the quiet ones.
But no one ever warned you
that silence isn't the same as softness.
I've been quiet my whole life,
like a storm hiding behind a cloud,
waiting for the right moment to break free.

I've been the calm,
the still,
the space between words,
watching the world rush by
like they don't know
the thunder I carry inside me.
Like they don't feel the weight
of everything I've kept locked away.

They say,
watch out for the quiet ones.
But they only know half the story.
What they don't see
is the power in restraint,
the strength in holding back
when everything inside me screams
to break,
to shout,
to tear down the walls.
I've been quiet,
but not because I don't know how to speak.

I've been quiet
because I've learned the art of waiting—
waiting for the moment when my silence
becomes the loudest thing in the room.

I've been quiet,
and the world has tested me,
pushed me,
poked at my stillness
until they forgot
I was anything more than calm.
Until they didn't see
the beast beneath the surface.
The woman who will rise,
unleashed,
fierce,
when I'm finally pushed too far.
But I don't want to be her.
I don't want to be the one who explodes.
I don't want to break the silence,
only to realize I can't control the pieces I've shattered.

So, I pray.
Jehovah,
teach me patience,
teach me strength in silence.
Hold me steady when the world demands
I speak louder than my peace.
Guide me through the chaos
without letting me lose my calm.
Let me choose
who I become,
not the world.

But they don't understand.
They don't know that silence
isn't weakness.
It's a choice.
It's a weapon.
And I've been quiet
long enough to know

when to use it.
Rishawna L. Gould

Black-eyed Companion

I crave the hush of solitude
Longing for silence, no expectations, no need to explain presence or lack of it

I walk away to find myself,
but leave breadcrumbs
just in case someone cares to follow

Each crumb soaked in silent pleas
Echoing unheard
I guess I should stop being disappointed when it leads to a trail of tears
Stained in bloodthirsty fears
Of being left behind in the land of the forgotten

Only companion: the Raven

Black-eyed and patient
Solemn in its dark beauty

Gnawing at what remains of the spine of my restraint

Somersaulting off my air of doubts
That the taste of isolation won't linger

Yearning for the sound of footsteps to echo behind me

Gentle, sure, proud, present

Now only wings
And the crunch of forgetting

I wrap myself in shadows,
not for comfort,
but because they don't leave

And even the Raven,
with its hunger,
at least believes I'm real enough to grieve.
AlexaBAD

For Bryan
(Ernie)

Today I met grief.
We've brushed shoulders a few times with the passing of other family members and friends but today grief and I embrace.

My heart feels ten times heavier, and I fear it will
shatter under this loss.
This loss feels like a part of my soul has been ripped away, tossed to the winds of wails and tears.

Nothing compares to the loss of a child but to lose a sibling feels like a close second.
I've watched you grow from a distance but even at arm's length
that brother-sister bond was always there unbreakable and full of love.

I would've fought for you until we were the
last ones standing.
I would've died for you so you can be here to raise your children.

Now, I will cry for you and hold your memory so close to my chest nothing on this earth can take it from
me.
I treasure that the last words we said to each other were "I love you, Bro" and you said, "I love
you, Sis" with that big, beautiful smile on your face that could melt any heart because it always
melted mine.

Even with the hope of seeing you again
this pain that is felt today is one I would never wish upon an enemy.

The crushing of my soul and the never-ending tear flow because I can't hug you in this moment is beyond devastating.

I wish this wasn't our reality.
I hear your laugh when I close my eyes, and I want to keep them closed
so I can just hear your laugh over
and over on repeat.

At some point I have to open them and accept that you're gone for
now.
Till we meet again
I love you, my sweet little brother,
we may have lost you, but we will never
forget you.
Vita Gold

Lukewarm

Numbness brings calmness and dissatisfaction
I'm not a fraction of who I was before
I don't know who I prefer more

Decisive is inviting
Impulsive is exciting
Just depends on the lighting in the room

Silent daggers stagger across the room
Eyes presumed dead
Read:
Save me
Save me from this cocktail of "Let's Get Well"
Drunk on sanity

Ideas cradle the grave of my tears
Album drops will stop
There is no life after death

My eye won't drift to the left
My pen won't follow

What will I write about tomorrow?

And the day after
There's no laughter
There's no weeping

I'm just steeping in a pot of lukewarm lava
I mean water

'Cause there is no fire
No desire
No motivation
There's just medication

Pills kill Thrill's feels
Like nothing at all
Sophia Monet

relief

there be other poems leadin to this one
just like there be other ways gettin to this need of relief
i see them on faces of other children
my grown friends
who miss they mommas
who ain't recovered yet
whose grief
sour like bad breath
and won't brush away
but they keep gettin up each day
swallowin they pain
and memories like medicine
tryin to numb the howlin wind that replaces conversations
and laughter

they an example i don't want to follow
not because it ain't good
the way they cleared out rooms/ for they Momma's things/ rearranged schedules so she never alone/ sacrificin salt/ fried chicken/ potato chips and beer/ 'cause she can't have none of that/ and denyin her be worse than sayin no to a baby

she became my baby

that i watched while she slept
between rounds of computer games and the news
and if she wasn't on the couch she was on her bed
so my ears learned to hear her over the white noise that sang in the stairwell and down the hallway separatin us
and i wonder how she was able to watch us leave home for school/ for ministry/ for marriage and not worry herself into the knot that's growin big/ like tumor of a still born anxiety about her leavin

me

i don't want any examples of how to do this
how to say goodbye/ and feel relieved that she ain't sufferin/ and wow
didn't she have a long life
i don't want to join the just a little while longer club

but i can't find a way off this conveyor belt

it only rides in one direction
you fallin off is going to happen
sooner than later

there is no healin from old age
without Jehovah
who will place his surgical hands on us
on you
when he gets ready
and he may have to collect you from
a deep sleep
but he don't have to hear you
to know you still there
no hallway too long
or a stairwell too steep
to retrieve you

i know his promises he will keep

you will rise
if you make the leap

it's just that you dying now
ain't a relief

not to me
Terri Boyd-Boone

Severed

Severed

I'm thankful this isn't forever
Won't produce more fruit this side of truth
Yet still trying to keep it together
Scars reveal what hasn't truly healed

Missing a carriage

I grin and bear it
But, knowing only two will inherit cuts deep
Knowing it should be 3

Sliced

Up all night thinking just what might have been
Then relief mixed with grief sets in

It's that exhale knowing very well it would have very well been overwhelming
That's an understatement
But under that statement comes a piercing knife

A loss a life

Well not quite
A bit underdeveloped
Like these tears that swell up
Decision making no more belly aching
Severed ties with my own insides
Sophia Monet

She Let Him Hurt Me

You were my sister.
The one I trusted.
The one I loved without question.
I was just a girl —
and you were supposed to be my shield.
But when he raised his hand to me —
you watched.
And you told me,
"Don't tell Mom and Dad."
"Don't ruin the wedding."
"Don't make it about you."
And I didn't.
I swallowed that pain whole,
choked on silence
so your day could be beautiful.
So you wouldn't lose anything.
He did it again.
After you were his wife.
And again —
you said nothing.
Again —
you turned away.
Again —
you chose **him.**
I was your little sister.
Your **blood**.
Your childhood memory.
Your shadow.
And you gave me to him
like I was nothing.
Like I was disposable.
Like my bruises were just
inconvenient background noise.
And now?

Years later.
After the marriage
crumbled into dust,
after he's long gone —
you laugh,
you joke,
you talk to me like
none of it happened.
Like you didn't make me promise
to keep quiet.
Like I was never terrified.
Never shaking.
Never fifteen and begging silently
for my big sister to see me.
But I do.
I remember everything.
And it wasn't just what he did.
It was what *you didn't do.*
It was your silence
that carved the deepest scar.
It was the way you
saw me,
and still
looked away.
You sacrificed me.
And all I ever wanted
was for you to say:
"I'm sorry I didn't protect you."
"I'm your sister. I should have acted like one."
But you never did.
Maybe you never will.

People say:
"*It's been 20 years.*"
"*Let it go.*"

But they weren't there.
They weren't in that room.
They didn't hear your silence
as loud as his hands **grabbing me** and **body slamming me** to the ground or **yanking me** up by my collar.
They didn't watch you
choose him.
Twice.
I've healed.
Not because of you.
But in spite of you.

I don't need anything from you now.
Not your truth.
Not your apology.

I forgive you —
because I refuse to carry
your shame
in my bones anymore.

But don't mistake my peace
for reunion.
You are my sister.
By blood.
That's all.

I needed you then.
And you weren't there.
So now —
I'm good.
Not bitter.
Just free.
But I will never forget.
Because some betrayals
don't fade with time.

They echo —
in the silence
where love
should have been.
Rishawna L. Gould

For the One Who Stayed Up

For the one who stayed up

Moon asks not if you need light amongst the darkness
She simply shines,
illuminates
Casting light even on the hidden things

You,
your radiation clearly dependent not on spotlight
You spotlight fading
You supply the one from He to make up the difference
You
set the mood
Though they grieve their strength
You console spirit

You,
with the steady hands and tired eyes,
who learned to read pain like second language—
You,
you've done enough

Where others saw nonsensical dots connecting you to adulthood
It was
You,
Touching a life like Braille
Amidst feeling your way through existence
fingertips grasping on to yours for dear life

You were the calm in their storm while trying not to drown in your own tsunami

You,
you were candle
Sweet incense lighting the way to hopeful beginnings,

leaving the scent of what used to feel like home—
While their fragility imprisoned them
in their woes

You,
you burned on both ends and still managed to warm someone else

I know it feels as if that spark is dimming
Never forget
You,
You are fire

You cannot fuel them until you breathe

You've carried the weight of the world
on borrowed power—
You've never been more powerful
Through every prayer you prayed in silence and every tear He heard
you cry in hiding
His skin bottle full of blessings
To pour out on your kintsugi heart
Molded with His signature touch

You are not weakest link
The week is linked
to all the days you've endured
that of which to the world is unseen
The late nights
Those moments where your presence softened their loneliness
Where the cups of tea, you stirred with warmth, held with care, melted
away their angst

Where no one saw the strength it took to roll out of bed to care for
them, when self-caring to rise another day was an uncharted feeling
mapped in detriment

Love measured in refilled prescriptions and reheated meals—
Still counted worthy in crumbs

Even the dogs wait beneath the table for mercy to fall,

So, you knelt—not as lesser, but as listener for those feeling unheard
Heart cupped open, still praying heals
Heals.
Now **You...**
Heel.
Heal.

The blessing comes to those who persist

Angels took note
Midheaven
They noticed the days your ministry was in-home
It starts there
So, you kept knocking
For enough courage for two

You,
you walked with Weakness clinging to your side,
a great weight to bear
Even when you cracked you never dropped what you carried

Now may your heavy heart be lifted
May the handle be opened to Hope,
who waits with open arms,
knees bent,
ready to hoist your weary soul

For the One Who Stayed Up
Inhale
Exhale
Repeat

Yes, **You**
Breathe
Let Weight slip from your shoulders
She clings, stubborn-fingered,
whispers of "not yet,"
Let Him tell her,
"Enough"

Disrobe worries
who drapes herself in tomorrows, fawns over sunsets,
and tiptoes through your chest at night

You,
Your battle has not gone unnoticed
You've fought well
The One who sees all
Whether it be during light of day or darkness of night

has already prepared a quiet crown
Not for fame—
for faith

Not for applause—
but for
how you stayed
when no one clapped

May Peace meet you not as stranger,
but as old friend who has sat with you in the silence
all along
Holding your hand through every still moment
Yes, For the One Who Stayed Up
Heel
Heal
AlexaBAD

missed

we are new/ we met too late
i missed the playground installation of nicknames and being introduced as
oh this is Timmy's little friend
the plus one on family vacation
we missed the eye witness/ of back in the day/ now on replay/ of how you got that scar/ and conversations that start with *remember that time*

because it was before my time with you

i missed the morphing moments
becoming play cousins and how your momma's best friend is your auntie
so I've forged permission slips for field trips
to archives of purple dreams and ocean wave memories

i stole the key to your journal that holds your origin story
and i wonder how to be an old pal when/ we are still unwrapped with price tags attached/ when all i want is to feel like that raggedy baby blanket/ or worn-out teddy bear that survived your nightmares

i want to be grandfathered into this family tree so nothing after this happens without me
because when we met it was instant
a flashback a hologram of sorts

wasn't i there
wasn't i flesh

should we do it the old school way
cut fingers and be blood related
rub some dirt on me to take the new shine off/ wash me over and over
to feel like a favorite pair of jeans

did i miss my chance
not to be thrown away
just because

we met too late to be old friends
by now
Terri Boyd-Boone

all weight ain't heavy

(to my Tuddah and my Lenny Penny)

love is a weight
it ain't always heavy
it anchors me to a sistering space

it is pajama days
and joke time
sucking on jawbreakers while playing spades

it is a warm coat
thick wool long sleeves cozy
it wraps me up and lets me float

it is a gift in many boxes
hard for a two handed carry
so sorry sometimes i drop them

it is new understanding
wrapped in forgiving
tied around the truth

it is simple
it is clear
it taping from the radio
while writing out lyrics
learning words to our favorite songs

it is 2nd helpings of a favorite meal
it makes you rub your belly
after popping open a button
becoming comfortable being full

love is a weight
but it aint always heavy

friends forever
it anchors me to you in this place
Terri Boyd-Boone

Daddy

In this moment I became a man.
The first one to protect you from the evils of this world.
The road was never easy because it wasn't easy for me.
With the examples I had, I tried to be your dad
with shabby tools I did my best to raise the woman I'm proud to call
Daughter.
You gave me my first grey hairs and many more would follow.
Through fights and tears
if I knew what the teenage
years would be I may have done things a bit differently.
I would've married a woman who would've and should've
loved you as much as I do.
I would've given you the truth sooner
before you suffered your first heartbreak.
Of all the things I could and would do differently raising you is still my greatest accomplishment.
You are truly my pride and joy, my one and only baby girl.
In these arms you are
always home no matter where you go.
Vita Gold

big mama say

y'all come on

navy beans 'n cornbread
every meal a reunion
sweet yellow onions
'n garlic garlic garlic

hands sort beans
lookin fo rocks
fixin to be creamy white
wid a taste of fat ham hocks

got us hootin 'n singin 'n sharin
til somebody say *oh ma glory*
tellin all da bidnez
not seasoned wid tact
den pray fo forgiveness
ova dis here chit chat

house swellin wid grandma's recipes
like da size of a big mama's waist
house smellin oh so scrumptiously
makin my mouth water 'n impatiently wait

measure da flour
measure da corn
sprinkle some sugar
girl you betta add some mo'

roast some ham render da lard
try not to taste too much
greasy smackin fingers
oh ma lawd

navy beans 'n cornbread

served hot wid luv
it's a simple plate
big mama hands on big hips
say

come here baby
would you like a taste
Terri Boyd-Boone

elephant's foot

(for Timbre)

i chose you because
you are like watching a favorite tv show
over and over
and still laughing even though
i know all the jokes

i chose you because
you are like a redwood tree
your roots entangle with mine
and run a distance towards good water
for the branches one day we will conceive

i chose you because
you are safe and you are kind
you accept all the versions
i sing of myself and
you remove the heavy elephant foot
of my mind

i choose you
and will do
each day until the end of time
Terri Boyd-Boone

Grits

My grandmother's kitchen smelled like porcelain and Palmolive
A combination I never knew I needed in my life
But, down to this day it makes everything right
Quite...
Like...
She did

A skinned knee
A bruised elbow
Hurt feelings

She offered healing

Her words ran long
Like a Luther song
A house ain't a home without granny in the front room

Pressing the naps
And cleaning the nape
Always willing to wait
Until I fell asleep to make my heart feel complete and safe

Us on that bus
Never in a rush
Just full of trust and admiration
Prepared for every situation

Solid

She got it taken care of
Before it even happened

I watched her pull weeds from her garden with her bare hands
That's how I knew she would understand what it meant to be in the thick of it

Never let it show when she was sick of it
They don't make em like her anymore

Face to the floor
I pray for a taste of her grace and a pinch of her patience

And the recipe to her grits
Sophia Monet

Heirloom

The weight I wear around this neck laced with bitter regret cause and effect
I didn't expect this outcome
I didn't expect you to be gone so young
This heirloom came too soon too quick
Didn't want your story to be over with
Now I'm left wearing it
The air that looms over my heart
Left in the dark
From unfinished conversations trying not to drown in frustration
As grief greets my feet at the turning of the door
At the turning of the seasons
Please give me a reason to keep going on without you
My hand rest on my chest slow caress of your necklace
I miss you
Sophia Monet

if i should go

(for Edith and my girls)

if i should go
before the next time we talk
remember the time i told you

i love you

and if i didn't say it in a way
that could now d
              a
              n
              g
              l
              e
from the rear view mirror of your mind
or neglected to place it like a bumper sticker
so everyone would know how i feel about you

i love you

wait/

can't you hear my voice

telling you things about yourself
that only someone who loves you would notice
and keep close/ protected/ handy like an aunty's hanky passed down
from her Momma/ but never used/
i keep your details folded down near my bosom
in the pocket of my heart

i know i said i love you

but maybe you dismissed it because sometimes

i talk too LOUD
and stay too l o n g at the kitchen table
so you got to wondering when was i going home
instead of listening to me
but i hope you know/ you were my home/ your couch was my therapy/
your ears were a file cabinet i could stash my secrets and insecurities in

so hey/
don't think about the words
just remember the hugs
ok

and if i didn't hug you
and linger
tightly
in a way that still squeezes
with each inhale
did we at least hold hands like school kids?
you could get away with that in the sandbox/ between turns on the
swing/ between *Miss Mary Mac Mac Mac all dressed in black black
black/ and down down baby down by the roller coaster*
you see
i feel innocent and playground young with you
even though times are different
and we old now
i know i wanted to be your bestest friend
and maybe you didn't like to be squeezed too much
my love languages generally don't understand personal space politics

but i love you like i said i did

so i kept my hands to myself
except when i touched your mind with a poem i stashed in my laugh
don't you remember how we sure liked to laugh
over the cake saved for after everyone left

and if i didn't laugh
in a way that sounded like a favorite song
you could play over and over now that i'm gone
making up lyrics as you sing along
or how we could talk for hours on the phone
or in the car/ in front of the house we were supposed to visit
us giggling like slumber parties
whispering when we knew better and someone gave us the side eye/ twice

just remember the blue skies of my smile

the reflection of the sunshine you brought in my day
like warm rays
especially when my life was shades of grey
and by the way
i'm sorry for the rain showers following me like Schleprock/ having me sounding like Eeyore/ got you all wet because you never closed your door on me/ standing close sharing scriptures/ and Jehovah/ and promises
and reminding me about myself

oh
you were telling me that you loved me

i knew that
just like i know i showed you/ told you

i love you

so please remember that
if i should go
before the next time we talk
Terri Boyd-Boone

the weight we wear

these days are dragged down heavy days
these days are tired and lonely days
these days are more memories than living days
these are uncertain days
these are frustrating days
these are scared for our children days
and hope we make it home days
these are please give me more faith days
these days are overweight
overloaded and overburdened days
these are overthinking
overwhelming over my head days
and some days feel like too much

but we are like Moses
remember the help we have to hold our hands up

my love
we have 4 hands and one flesh between us
we can carry it

my sisters of the soul
we have the 6 hands we held between us
we can carry it

my cuzz and cuzzos and cousins
we have more than hands and long summers between us
we can carry it

Mommy Auntie Uncles
add your 8 hands to all our hands
you nursed taught and legacy-ed us to understand
we have more hands between us
so we can carry it

my big brothers and baby brothers
my spiritual fathers and second mothers
my special sisters and all my children
we are stitched together shoulder-to-shoulder
to carry wheelbarrows of each other's purple triangles and die for each other
in Russia and Eritrea
Singapore and South Korea
Ukraine and Crimea
reaching hands through bars for you
we pray for you
we can't even count the number of hands between us

but raise them
and raise your eyes
see the flames
count the sand

most of all
add the Almighty's big hand
and the one that sits on his right hand
because of them
we have walked on water
we will stand again

we can carry it
yes
we can carry it
Terri Boyd-Boone

About the Authors

Sophia Monet
Sophia Monet is a dynamic and innovative writer whose work captivates readers with its raw honesty and imaginative flair. As a passionate storyteller, Sophia delves into the intricacies of life, embracing themes of creativity, resilience, and the pursuit of authenticity. Her unique perspective and vibrant voice shine through in her writing, making her an exciting contributor to the upcoming anthology. Sophia's ability to be candid and vulnerable with deep emotional insight invites readers to explore their own narratives and challenges. Connect with her journey and creative endeavors on Instagram at [@creativelyinsanebutimnotstupid](https://www.instagram.com/creativelyinsanebutimnotstupid/) and listen to "My Own Name" available on Audiomack to experience her captivating world of words and inspiration.

Rishawna L. Gould

Rishawna L. Gould is an author and poet born in Washington, DC. whose words rise from the sacred places of lived experience. Guided by unwavering faith in her Heavenly Father, she writes to heal, to honor her journey, and to remind others that even in the breaking, there is beauty. Her poetry gives voice to the tender spaces of love and lost love, heartbreak and healing, rebirth and resilience—testimonies of endurance, hope, and the quiet strength found on the other side of surrender.

The love of traveling is an addictive pastime for Rishawna - both a movement and a journey of education, where each step unfolds new lessons in culture, history, and the shared human experience. A living classroom where lessons reach far beyond geography and deep into the language of humanity, culture, and creation. She believes that through exposure, education, and the courage to step beyond what is known, people can discover not only the world—but the extraordinary power within themselves.

As a resilient stroke survivor and full-time graphic designer, Rishawna carries each day as a gift. Whether through illustration, advocacy, or the soft landing of a poem on paper, she creates from a place of purpose, grace, and gratitude—forever walking by faith, not by sight. She currently lives in Laurel, MD.

Vita Gold

JoVita (Vita Gold) Goldsby is a performing poet who began writing at the age of twelve and first graced the stage at a high school talent show. Since then, their passion for poetry has grown into a powerful performing art, capturing audiences with each word. JoVita became a regular at The B-Side, one of Cleveland, OH's most popular poetry nights, where their electrifying performances earned them a loyal following. They've also showcased their talent in Atlanta, further expanding their reach. With a focus on themes of life changes, personal growth, and love, JoVita continues to bring poetry to life, one performance at a time.

Instagram-@vitachari | Facebook- JoVita Goldsby

Terri Boyd-Boone

Terri Boyd-Boone is a talented writer and poet known for her evocative and thought-provoking contributions to the literary world and much of her work lives at the intersection of memory, music, family, and emotion. Terri's poems are shaped by nostalgia, by the landscapes of childhood, and by the layered language of inheritance—what we carry, what we mourn, what we keep alive in rhythm and line. She writes to hold on to things that don't have names, to honor the people who raised her, and to give voice to experiences that shaped her own sense of belonging and becoming. After completing her undergraduate in English, Terri's emergence as a published poet began with the Train River Poetry: Summer 2020 Anthology, but her roots go deeper—Terri was previously published in The Reading and Writing of African American Poetry by UC Berkeley Students (1990) and Afrikan Student Literary Magazine (1991). Drawing on her rich background and diverse experiences, she crafts powerful narratives that invite reflection and connection. As she prepares to contribute to an upcoming anthology, Terri continues to inspire through her words, encouraging others to embrace their own journeys and share their stories. Follow her creative journey on Instagram at [@i.used.2.b.a.poet](https://www.instagram.com/i.used.2.b.a.poet/) to stay updated on her latest projects and insights.

AlexaBAD

AlexaBAD is a compelling voice in contemporary literature, known for her fearless expression and thought-provoking insights. With a passion for storytelling that breaks boundaries, AlexaBAD explores themes of identity, empowerment, and social justice in her writing. Her contributions to the upcoming anthology promise to resonate deeply with readers, as she masterfully intertwines personal experiences with broader societal narratives. Known for her vibrant personality and creativity, AlexaBAD invites her audience to embrace truth and challenge the status quo. Follow her journey and discover her powerful work on Instagram at [@al3xa_unleashed](https://www.instagram.com/al3xa_unleashed/) and spotify to stay updated on her latest projects and inspirations.

Authors' Literary Works By Title

AlexaBAD
Beneath the Hyde...Seek
Genius to Madness
Listen to the Fire
The Weight Mistaken for Me
Tulips
Force of Nature
Hands That Listen
Open Arms, Closed Doors
Black-eyed Companion
For the One Who Stayed Up

Rishawna L. Gould
Ashes of the Unapologetic
Say It Again, So I Believe You
The Beast I Keep Locked In
The Echoes Before Hello
The Weight of Wings
"You Still Sick?"
I'm Going To Paint Me A Picture
Watch Out for the Quiet Ones
It Took Her. It Tried Me.
She Let Him Hurt Me

Terri Boyd-Boone
gorda
letting go
pushing past my crust relief
missed
all weight ain't heavy
big mama say
elephant's foot (for Timbre)
if I should go (for Edith and my girls)
the weight we wear

Sophia Monet
Air
Home Me
PTSD
Sackcloth and Ashes
The Wait We Bear
Gravity
Lukewarm
Severed
Grits
Heirloom

Vita Gold
Beware (Proverbs 7)
Freedom
In Your Eye
Jesus Got Me Thinking
Stripped
A Walk in the Rain
Decisions
She
For Bryan (Ernie)
Daddy

www.ingramcontent.com/pod-product-compliance
Lightning Source LLC
Chambersburg PA
CBHW060838190426
43197CB00040B/2678